OGH

AN IRISH A

Is córas scríbhneoireachta Gaeilge an tOgham. Córas diamhair atá ann a bhí in úsáid go tréan mar mheán cumarsáide faoin cheathrú céad. Ní fios cé a chum an tOgham ná fiú cén uair a cumadh é ach, de réir na miotaseolaíochta, ba é an dia Ceilteach Ogmios, dia na hurlabhra agus na foghlama, a cheap.

Is amhlaidh atá tréithe d'aibítir na Laidine le sonrú ar an Ogham. Tá fiche litir ar fad in aibítir an Oghaim agus stríoca agus poncanna mar bhunús leo. Tá an aibítir curtha in oiriúint do scríbhinn ar líne ingearach, mar a bheadh ar chiumhais chloiche. Córas poncanna do na gutaí agus córas stríoc do na consain atá ann. Ghearrtaí na poncanna ar lárlíne ar a dtugtaí 'fleasc' agus ghearrtaí na stríoca trasna na líne sin, nó ar an taobh deas den líne, nó ar an taobh clé. Is gnách gur aníos a léitear an tOgham.

The curious form of Irish known as Ogham is very old, being well established as a medium of written communication by the fourth century. No one knows when or by whom the Ogham alphabet was invented but scholars believe that it originated in Ireland. According to mythology it is attributed to Ogmios, the Celtic God of speech and oral learning.

Ogham bears influences of the Latin alphabet and consists of twenty letters each signified by one or more lines or notches carved along a verticle line, for example along the edge of a standing stone. The lines represent consonants and the notches vowels. The notches were cut onto the centre line which was known as a 'fleasc'. The lines were cut across, to the right or to the left of the centre line. As a general rule Ogham is read from the bottom upwards.

Cé go ndéantar tagairt i luathscríbhinní na nGael do dhaoine a bhain feidhm as an Ogham le horthaí a scríobh ar adhmad agus ar chnámh, níl le fáil inniu ach roinnt samplaí atá greanta ar chlocha, agus fosta ar roinnt bheag lámhdhéantúsán - ina measc, bróiste airgid atá le feiceáil in Iarsmalann Náisiúnta na hÉireann. Is amhlaidh atá bunús na gcloch greanta suite in iardheisceart na hÉireann. Tá clocha Oghaim le fáil sa Bhreatain fosta agus is i nGaeilge atá scríbhinní Oghaim na gcloch sin ach gur minic a bhíonn leaganacha Laidine scríofa i gcarachtair Rómhánacha le fáil lena gcois.

Bhain Piochtaí thuaisceart na hAlban feidhm as an Ogham gur scríobh a dteanga féin ar ghalláin atá le feiceáil go fóill. Ar an drochuair ní féidir an teanga sin a thuiscint anois.

Is clocha cuimhneacháin bunús na gcloch Oghaim a bhfuil eolas ar fáil fúthu. Níl scríofa ar na clocha sin ach ainm an mhairbh. Is í teanga na n-inscríbhinní Oghaim an leagan is ársa den Ghaeilge dá bhfuil ann.

Although early literature refers to charms being written on bone and timber, the only surviving evidence of Ogham exists on pillar-stones and on a small number of artefacts including, for example, a silver brooch which can be seen in the National Museum of Ireland. The majority of the inscribed stones are to be found in the south-west of Ireland. Ogham stones also exist in Britain where the Irish written in Ogham is often accompanied by a Latin inscription in Roman characters.

The Picts of northern Scotland used Ogham and wrote their own language on standing stones which are still to be seen. Unfortunately the key to this language is now lost.

For the most part, known Ogham inscriptions are commemorative of important persons. The language of the inscriptions is the earliest attested form of Irish.

Maíonn roinnt scríbhneoirí gur siombailí draíochta atá san Ogham, siombailí a raibh baint acu le deasghnátha na ndraoithe. Saoithe agus sagairt shochaí na gCeilteach a bhí sna draoithe agus bhí ceangal láidir idir an dúlra agus an reiligiún acu. Chreidtí go forleathan go mbíodh cumhachtaí osnádúrtha ag na draoithe céanna.

Cuid den tsiocair a meastar go bhfuil baint ag an Ogham leis an draíocht ná go bhfuil nasc idir a chuid siombailí agus an dúlra. Is amhlaidh atá ainm faoi leith ar gach ceann de charachtair an Oghaim agus is minic gur ainm crainn atá ann. Mar shampla, is é ainm chéad litir aibítir an Oghaim ná 'beith', lena bhfuil an chiall 'beith' nó 'crann beithe' i nGaeilge an lae inniu. Is ar an ábhar sin a tharlaíonn gur minic a thugtar 'aibítir na gcrann' ar aibítir an Oghaim.

T hat Ogham is a series of magical symbols has been suggested by some writers who claim its links with druidic rights. The druids were the learned caste or priestly profession in Celtic society and their religion was particularly nature-orientated. It was believed that they had mystical powers and could use their learning to perform magic.

Part of the reason for Ogham's association with magic is the relation between its symbols and nature. Each of the Ogham characters has a name. Most of these names refer to trees. For example, the first letter of the Ogham alphabet, the letter 'b', is known as 'beith' meaning 'a birch tree'. For this reason Ogham is sometimes referred to as 'the tree alphabet'.

Is amhlaidh a bhí stádas faoi leith ag baint le crainn sa tsochaí Cheilteach agus go háirithe i measc na ndraoithe. Bhí tábhacht faoi leith ag an chrann darach i measc na ndraoithe. Creideann scoláirí áirithe gur as fréamh an fhocail 'dair' a d'eascair an focal 'draoi'. Is é 'dair' ainm an tseachtú litir, an litir 'd', d'aibítir an Oghaim.

Chreid na Gaeil go mbíodh tábhacht naofa ag baint le seanchrainn áirithe. Thugtaí 'bile' ar a leithéid de chrann. Maireann an t-ainm sin go fóill i logainmneacha éagsúla, mar shampla Maigh Bhile (Contae an Dúin) agus Ráth Bhile (Contae Cheatharlach.)

De réir dhlíthe na mBreithiún, ghearrtaí fíneáil ar dhuine as dochar a dhéanamh do chrann. Ghearrtaí an pionós sin de réir an díobháil a bhí déanta. Dá mbaintí géag de chrann, ghearrtaí colpach mar éiric. Ghearrtaí bó bhainne mar fhíneáil as stoc crainn a ghearradh.

Trees had a very important place in Celtic society and particularly among the druids. Of particular importance to this learned class was the oak tree or 'dair'. Some scholars hold that the word 'druid' is derived from this tree name. 'Dair' is the term attributed to the seventh letter, the letter 'd', of the Ogham alphabet.

The belief long survived among the Celtic people that a very old or notable tree was sacred. In Ireland such trees were known as 'bile' and are commemorated in placenames such as Maigh Bhile (Moville, Co.Down) and Ráth Bhile (Rathvilly, Co.Carlow).

According to Brehon Law, which was the common law of Ireland until the sixteenth century, a fine was incurred by those who damaged trees. Restitution was made in accordance to the damage caused. If a branch was severed, a yearling heifer was to be paid. If the tree was cut at the base, a milch-cow was to be forfeited.

Déantar tagairt don bhaint seo idir an crann agus an tOgham go mion minic i litríocht na nGael. Sa tseanscríbhinn 'Uraiceacht na nÉigeas' tugtar léargas ar conas an tOgham a léamh:

'Is amlaidh im-drengar Ogum amal im-drengar crann .i. saltrad fora frem in chroinn ar tus - do lam dess remut - do lam cle fo deoid. Is iar-sin is leis - is fris- is trit - is immi.'

'Dreaptar Ogham faoi mar a dhreaptar crann, i.e. seasamh ar fhréamh an chrainn ar dtús, do lámh dheas romhat amach, do lámh chlé ar deireadh. Ina dhiaidh sin is thairis, ina aghaidh, tríd agus timpeall air (a théitear).'

The association between the tree and Ogham is repeatedly highlighted in Irish texts. One manuscript, 'Auraicept na nÉces' (The Scholars' Primer), provides the following instructions for reading Ogham:

'Is amlaidh im-drengar Ogum amal im-drengar crann .i. saltrad fora frem in chroinn ar tus - do lam dess remut - do lam cle fo deoid. Is iar-sin is leis - is fris- is trit - is immi.'

'Ogham is climbed as a tree is climbed; by treading on the root of the tree first with one's right hand before one and one's left hand last. After that it is across it and against it and through it and around it (one goes).'

Faightear tagairtí do chumhachtaí draíochta an Oghaim sa bhéaloideas. Ríomhtar scéal faoi thaisce a aimsíodh faoi chrann darach i ndiaidh d'fheirmeoir brionglóid a bheith aige go raibh sí ann. Faoin taisce féin bhí cloch ina luí agus roinnt marcanna aisteacha greanta uirthi nach raibh aon duine ábalta ciall a bhaint astu. Blianta ina dhiaidh tháinig scoláire bocht taistil chun an cheantair gur fiafraíodh de an raibh sé in ann marcanna na cloiche a thuiscint. Léigh an scoláire:

"Más maith an taobh seo is fearr go mór an taobh eile."

I ndiaidh leaba na cloiche a chuardach an athuair fuarthas an dá oiread taisce agus a fuarthas an chéad uair agus í ina luí san áit inar aimsíodh an chloch. Is cinnte nach dtiocfaí go deo ar an taisce seo ach ab é tuiscint an scoláire ar an aibítir ársa.

In folklore Ogham is often cited as a mystical form of communication. One popular legend tells of how treasure was discovered under an oak tree after a farmer dreamt of finding it there. At the base of the treasure lay a stone on which there were strange markings which no one could decipher until, years later, a poor travelling scholar visited the district and was asked if he understood the marks. The scholar read:

"Más maith an taobh seo is fearr go mór an taobh eile."

"If this side is good the other side is far better."

After once more investigating the site where the stone was found, a second and greater store of treasure was discovered. This treasure would surely have been lost but for the scholar's knowledge of the ancient alphabet.

B

L

F

S

N

H

D

T

C

Q

G

Ng

Z

R

0

U

I

E

Ogum i llia, lia uas lecht,

bali i téigtis fecht fir,

mac ríg hErend ro gaet and

do gae gand os gabur gil.

Véarsa ó Leabhar Laighean

An Ogham stone, a stone over a grave,

in the place where men were wont to pass;

the son of the king of Ireland was there slain

by a mighty spear on a white horse's back.

A verse from The Book of Leinster

Breis Léitheoireachta

Is iomaí tuairim ag scoláirí i dtaobh chumadh an Oghaim agus i dtaobh na bhfeidhmeanna a baineadh as. Mar shampla, tá tagairtí le fáil i seanscríbhinní na meánaoiseanna a mhaíonn gur ainmníodh gach carachtar d'aibítir an Oghaim as crainn. Ní ghlacann scoláirí an lae inniu leis an bharúil sin áfach. Moltar na téacsanna a leanas mar bhreis léitheoireachta ar an ábhar:

Leabhar Bhaile an Mhóta, circa 1400, ina bhfuil léargas fíorspéisiúil ar an Ogham. Tá an lámhscríbhinn le feiceáil i Leabharlann Acadamh Ríoga na hÉireann, Baile Átha Cliath.

MacAlister,R.A.S. *Studies In Irish Epigraphy: a collection of revised readings of the ancient inscriptions of Ireland*, (Trí imleabhar), London,David Nutt,1897.

McManus,D. *A Guide To Ogham*, Maigh Nuad,An Sagart,1991.

O'Boyle,S. *Ogham: the poet's secret*, Dublin,Dalton,1980.

Sharkey,J. *Ogham Monuments In Wales*, Llanerch Publishers, 1992.

Further Reading

Scholars have suggested many varying ideas regarding Ogham, its origins and its uses. References exist in medieval texts, for example, to suggest that all of the characters of the Ogham alphabet are named after trees. However, this idea is not supported by contemporary scholars. The following texts are recommended for a detailed description of the subject:

Leabhar Bhaile an Mhóta (The Book of Ballymote) circa 1400, contains a fascinating account of Ogham. The manuscript is held in the library of the Royal Irish Academy, Dublin.

MacAlister,R.A.S. *Studies In Irish Epigraphy: a collection of revised readings of the ancient inscriptions of Ireland,* (Three volumes), London,David Nutt,1897.

McManus,D. *A Guide To Ogham,* Maigh Nuad,An Sagart,1991.

O'Boyle,S. *Ogham: the poet's secret,* Dublin,Dalton,1980.

Sharkey,J. *Ogham Monuments In Wales,* Llanerch Publishers, 1992.

Also of Interest from Hippocrene...

IRISH GRAMMAR: A BASIC HANDBOOK
Noel McGonagle
Students who are beginners, adults who need to brush up, or teachers in need of a trustworthy reference guide will welcome this handy, straightforward grammar handbook with its attractive format and easy-to-use approach.
Noel McGonagle is a lecturer in the Modern Irish Department in University College, Galway. He has written extensively on linguistic and literary aspects of Modern Irish.
100 pages • 5 ¼ x 7 ½ • 0-7818-0667-4 • $9.95pb • (759)

IRISH PROVERBS
Compiled by the Editors of Hippocrene
Illustrated by Fergus Lyons
A collection of wit and wisdom in the great oral tradition of Ireland makes this collection interesting and informative. Two hundred proverbs discuss the hard times, the good times and the great times experienced by the Irish people in the cities, out in the country, and by the sea. Also included are 30 illustrations from County Sligo artist Fergus Lyons, all of which add style and humor to the collection.
160 pages • 5 ½ x 8 ½ • 30 illustrations • 0-7818-0676-3 • $14.95hc • (761) • October 98

SCOTTISH PROVERBS
Compiled by the Editors of Hippocrene
Illustrated by Shona Grant
Through opinions of love, drinking, work, money, law and politics, the sharp wit and critical eye of the Scottish spirit is charmingly conveyed in this one-of-a-kind collection. The proverbs are listed in the colloquial Scots-English language of the turn-of-the-century with modern translations below. Included are twenty-five witty and playful illustrations. There is something for everyone in this collection.
130 pages • 6x 9 • 25 illustrations • 0-7818-0648-8 • $14.95 • W • (719) • May 1998

Love Poetry. . .

TREASURY OF IRISH LOVE POEMS, QUOTATIONS & PROVERBS
edited by Gabriel Rosenstock
This compilation of over 70 Irish love poems, quotations and proverbs spans 15 centuries and features English translations as well as poetry from such prominent Irish poets as Colin Breathnach and Nuala Ní Dhomhnaill. With selections exploring the realm of lost love, first love, and love's powerful grasp, discover why this book is essential to any Irish literature collection.
Gabriel Rosenstock is a noted Irish poet and translator. He wrote the introduction to Hippocrene's best-selling *Irish Love Poems: Dánta Grá.*
128 pages • 5 x 7 • 0-7818-06445 • $11.95hc • $11.95hc • (732)

IRISH LOVE POEMS: DÁNTA GRÁ
edited by Paula Redes
A beautifully illustrated anthology that offers an intriguing glimpse into the world of

Irish passion, often fraught simultaneously with both love and violence. For some contemporary poets this will be their first appearance in a U.S. anthology. Included are poets Thomas Moore, Padraic Pearse, W.B. Yates, John Montague, and Nuala Ni Dhomnaill.

Gabriel Rosenstock, famous poet and translator, forwards the book, wittily introducing the reader to both the collection and the rich Irish Poetic tradition.

176 pages • 6 x 9 • illustrated • 0-7818-0396-9 • $14.95 • (70)

SCOTTISH LOVE POEMS

A Personal Anthology

edited by Lady Antonia Fraser, re-issued edition

Lady Antonia Fraser has selected her favorite poets from Robert Burns to Aileen Campbell Nye and placed them together in a tender anthology of romance. Famous for her own literary talents, her critical writer's eye has allowed her to collect the best loves and passions of her fellow Scots into a book that will find a way to touch everyone's heart.

220 pages • 5 ½ x 8 ¼ • 0-7818-0406-x • $14.95pb • (482)

Language Guides...

IRISH-ENGLISH/ENGLISH-IRISH DICTIONARY AND PHRASEBOOK

This 1,400-word dictionary indicates pronunciation in English spelling and will swiftly acquaint visitors with a basic key vocabulary. Phrases cover travel, sightseeing, shopping and recreation. Plus notes are provided on grammar, pronunciation and dialect.

160 pages • 3 ¾ x 7 • 1,400 entries/phrases • 0-87052-110-1 NA • $7.95pb • (385)

SCOTTISH [DORIC]-ENGLISH/ENGLISH-SCOTTISH [DORIC] CONCISE DICTIONARY

Douglas Kynoch

This dictionary is a guide to the Scots language as spoken in parts of the northeastern corner of the country and northern England. Beginning with a brief introduction to spelling, pronunciation, and grammar it presents a two-way lexicon of North-East Scots with 12,000 significant entries.

186 pages • 5 ½ x 8 ½ • 12,000 entries • 0-7818-0655-0 • $12.95pb • (705) • September 98

SCOTTISH GAELIC-ENGLISH/ENGLISH-SCOTTISH GAELIC DICTIONARY

R. W. Renton & J.A. MacDonald

Scottish Gaelic is the language of a hearty, traditional people, over 75,000 strong. This dictionary provides the learner or traveler with a basic, modern vocabulary and the means to communicate in a quick fashion.

This dictionary includes 8,500 modern, up-to-date entries, a list of abbreviation and appendix of irregular verbs, a grammar guide, written especially for students and travelers.

416 pages • 5 ½ x 8 ½ • 0-7818-0316-0 • NA • $8.95pb • (285)

BEGINNER'S WELSH

Heini Gruffudd

The Welsh language, with its rich culture and heritage, has successfully survived to this day. More than half a million people speak the language throughout the country in

Wales, while thousands in England, the U.S. and elsewhere have continued to keep the language alive. Beginner's Welsh is an easy to follow guide to grammar, pronunciation and rules of the language. A clear and concise introduction to Welsh politics, the economy, literature, and geography preface the language guide.

Heini Gruffudd is an experienced teacher of Welsh. His best selling language books for adults are well-known in Wales. He currently works as a Welsh language and literature lecturer at the University of Wales, Swansea.

171 pages • 5 ½ x 8 ½ • 0-7818-0589-9 • W • $9.95pb • (712)

ETYMOLOGICAL DICTIONARY OF SCOTTISH-GAELIC
416 pages • 5 ½ x 8 ½ • 6,900 entries • 0-7818-0632-1 • $14.95pb • (710)

BRITISH-AMERICAN/AMERICAN-BRITISH DICTIONARY AND PHRASEBOOK
160 pages • 3 ¾ x 7 • 1,400 entries • 0-7818-0450-7 • W • $11.95pb • (247)

Travel Guides...

LANGUAGE AND TRAVEL GUIDE TO BRITAIN
266 pages • 5 ½ x 8 ½ • 2 maps, photos throughout, index • 0-7818-0290-3 • W • $14.95pb • (119)

Cookbooks...

Ireland
THE ART OF IRISH COOKING
Monica Sheridan
Nearly 200 recipes for traditional Irish fare.
166 pages • 5 ½ x 8 ½ • 0-7818-0454-X • W • $12.95pb • (335)

CELTIC COOKBOOK: Traditional Recipes from the Six Celtic Lands: Brittany, Cornwall, Ireland, Isle of Man, Scotland and Wales
Helen Smith-Twiddy
This collection of over 160 recipes from the Celtic world includes traditional, yet still popular dishes like Rabbit Hoggan and Gwydd y Dolig (Stuffed Goose in Red Wine).
200 pages • 5 ½ x 8 ½ • 0-7818-0579-1 • NA • $22.50hc (679)

New!
ENGLISH ROYAL COOKBOOK: FAVORITE COURT RECIPES
Elizabeth Craig
Dine like a King or Queen with this unique collection of over 350 favorite recipes of the English royals, spanning 500 years of feasts! Start off with delicate Duke of York Consommé as a first course, then savor King George the Fifth's Mutton Cutlets, and for a main course, feast on Quails à la Princess Louise in Regent's Plum Sauce, with Baked Potatoes Au Parmesan and Mary Queen of Scots Salad. For dessert, try a slice of Crown Jewel Cake, and wash it all down with a Princess Mary Cocktail. These are real recipes, the

majority of them left in their original wording. Although this book is primarily a cookery book, it can also be read as a revealing footnote to Court history. Charmingly illustrated throughout.

187 pages • 5 ½ x 8 ½ • 0-7818-0583-X • W • $11.95pb • (723) • May

Scotland
TRADITIONAL FOOD FROM SCOTLAND: THE EDINBURGH BOOK OF PLAIN COOKERY RECIPES

A delightful assortment of Scottish recipes and helpful hints for the home—this classic volume offers a window into another era.

336 pages • 5 ½ x 8 • 0-7818-0514-7 • W $11.95pb • (620)

Wales
TRADITIONAL FOOD FROM WALES
A Hippocrene Original Cookbook
Bobby Freeman

Welsh food and customs through the centuries. This book combines over 260 authentic, proven recipes with cultural and social history

332 pages • 5 ½ x 8 ½ • 0-7818-0527-9 • NA• $24.95 • (638)

TRADITIONAL RECIPES FROM OLD ENGLAND

Arranged by country, this charming classic features the favorite dishes and mealtime customs from across England, Scotland, Wales and Ireland.

28 pages • 5 x 8 ½ • 0-7818-0489-2 • W • $9.95pb • (157)

History . . .

NEW!
IRELAND: AN ILLUSTRATED HISTORY
Henry Weisser

While it is easy to appreciate the natural beauty of Ireland, the Emerald Isle's history is also a rich and complex subject of study. Spanning prehistoric and Celtic Ireland to modern times, this volume examines the people, religion, social changes and politics that have evolved into the tradition of moern Ireland. Henry Weisser takes the reader on a journey through Ireland's past - to show how historic events have left an indelible mark on everything from architecture and economy to the spirtit and lifestyles of the Irish people.

Henry Weisser received a Ph.D. from Columbia University and is a Professor of History at Colorado State University. He teaches Irish history and leads study tours of Ireland for American students. He is author of *Hippocrene Companion Guide to Ireland*, and *USA Guide to the Rocky Mountain States*.

130 pages • 5 x 7 • 50 illustrations • 0-7818-0693-3 • W • $11.95hc • November

All prices are subject to change. To order Hippocrene Books, contact your local bookstore, call (718) 454-2366, or write to : Hippocrene Books, 171 Madison Ave. New York, NY 10016. Please enclose check or money order adding $5.00 shipping (UPS) for the first book and $.50 for each additional title.